Practical
Pre-School

Planning
for Learning
through
Shapes

Rachel Sparks Linfield and Penny Coltman, illustrated by Cathy Hughes

Contents

Published by Step Forward Publishing Limited
35 Park Court, Park Street, Leamington Spa CV32 4QN Tel: 01926 420046
Step Forward Publishing Limited 1999
Planning for Learning through Shapes ISBN: 1 902438 14 0

Making plans

Why plan?

The purpose of planning is to make sure that all children enjoy a broad and balanced curriculum. All planning should be useful. Plans are working documents which you spend time preparing, but which should later repay your efforts. Try to be concise. This will help you in finding information quickly when you need it.

Long-term plans

Preparing a long-term plan, which maps out the curriculum during a year or even two, will help you to ensure that you are providing a variety of activities and are meeting statutory requirements of the Early Learning Goals (1999).

Your long-term plan need not be detailed. Divide the time period over which you are planning into fairly equal sections, such as half terms. Choose a topic for each section. Young children benefit from making links between the new ideas they encounter so as you select each topic, think about the time of year in which you plan to do it. A topic about minibeasts will not be very successful in November!

Although each topic will address all the areas of learning, some could focus on a specific area. For example, a topic on Shapes lends itself well to activities relating to mathematics. Another topic might particularly encourage the appreciation of stories. Try to make sure that you provide a variety of topics in your long-term plans.

Autumn 1	Colour
Autumn 2	Toys/Christmas
Spring 1	Spring
Spring 2	Shapes
Summer 1	Summer
Summer 2	Minibeasts

Medium-term plans

Medium-term plans will outline the contents of a topic in a little more detail. One way to start this process is by brainstorming on a large piece of paper. Work with your team writing down all the activities you can think of which are relevant to the topic. As you do this it may become clear that some activities go well together. Think about dividing them into themes. The topic of

Shapes, for example, has themes such as 'Holes', 'Tubes', 'Boxes' and 'Patterns'.

At this stage it is helpful to make a chart. Write the theme ideas down the side of the chart and put a different area of learning at the top of each column. Now you can insert your brainstormed ideas and quickly see where there are gaps. As you complete the chart take account of children's earlier experiences and provide opportunities for them to progress.

Refer back to the Early Learning Goals document and check that you have addressed as many different aspects of it as you can. Once all your medium-term plans are complete make sure that there are no neglected areas.

Day-to-day plans

The plans you make for each day will outline aspects such as:

- resources needed;

- the way in which you might introduce activities;

- the organisation of adult help;

- size of the group;

- timing.

Identify the learning which each activity is intended to promote. Make a note of any assessments or observations which you are likely to carry out. On your plans make notes of which activities were particularly successful, or any changes you would make another time.

Making plans

A final note

Planning should be seen as flexible. Not all groups meet every day, and not all children attend every day. Any part of the plan can be used independently, stretched over a longer period or condensed to meet the needs of any group. You will almost certainly adapt the activities as children respond to them in different ways and bring their own ideas, interests and enthusiasms. Be prepared to be flexible over timing as some ideas prove more popular than others. The important thing is to ensure that the children are provided with a varied and enjoyable curriculum which meets their individual developing needs.

Using the book

- Collect or prepare suggested resources as listed on page 21.

- Read the section which outlines links to the Early Learning Goals (pages 4 - 7) and explains the rationale for the topic of Shapes.

- For each weekly theme two activities are described in detail as an example to help you in your planning and preparation. Key vocabulary, questions and learning opportunities are identified.

- The skills chart on page 23 will help you to see at a glance which aspects of children's development are being addressed as a focus each week.

- As children take part in the Shapes topic activities, their learning will progress. 'Collecting evidence' on page 22 explains how you might monitor children's achievements.

- Find out on page 20 how the topic can be brought together in a grand finale involving parents, children and friends.

- There is additional material to support the working partnership of families and children in the form of a 'Home links' page, and a photocopiable 'Parent's page' found at the back of the book.

It is important to appreciate that the ideas presented in this book will only be a part of your planning. Many activities which will be taking place as routine in your group may not be mentioned. For example, it is assumed that sand, dough, water, puzzles, floor toys and large scale apparatus are part of the ongoing pre-school experience, as are the opportunities which increasing numbers of groups are able to offer for children to develop ICT skills. Role play areas, stories, rhymes and singing, and group discussion times are similarly assumed to be happening each week although they may not be a focus for described activities.

Using the Early Learning Goals

Having decided on your topic and made your medium-term plans you can use the Early Learning Goals to highlight the key learning opportunities your activities will address. The Early Learning Goals are split into six areas: Personal, Social and Emotional Development, Language and Literacy, Mathematics, Knowledge and Understanding of the World, Physical Development and Creative Development. Do not expect each of your topics to cover every goal but your long-term plans should allow for each child to work towards all of the goals.

The following section highlights parts of the Early Learning Goals document in point form to show what children are expected to be able to do by the time they enter Year 1 in each area of learning. These points will be used throughout this book to show how activities for a topic on Shapes link to these expectations. For example, Personal, Social and Emotional Development point 8 is 'work as part of a group or class taking turns'. Activities suggested which provide the opportunity for children to do this will have the reference PS8. This will enable you to see which parts of the Early Learning Goals are covered in a given week and plan for areas to be revisited and developed.

In addition you can ensure that activities offer variety in the outcomes to be encountered. Often a similar activity may be carried out to achieve different outcomes. For example, during this topic children make their own model village. They will be learning about materials as they make and describe their choices, discovering aspects of technology as they join pieces together and using early mathematical skills as they investigate and discuss aspects of shape and position. It is important therefore that activities have clearly defined learning outcomes so that these may be emphasised during the activity and for recording purposes.

Personal, Social and Emotional Development (PS)

This area of learning incorporates attitudes, skills and understanding and is a pre-condition for children's success in all other learning. The goals include children's personal, social, emotional, moral and spiritual development and the establishment of good attitudes to their learning.

By the end of the reception year most children should be:

PS1   confident to try things, initiate ideas and speak in a group

PS2   able to maintain attention, concentrate and sit still

PS3   interested, excited and motivated to learn

PS4   aware of their own needs, views and feelings and sensitive to the needs, views and feelings of others

PS5   respectful of their own cultures and beliefs and those of other people

PS6   responsive to significant experiences showing a range of feelings including joy, awe, wonder and sorrow

They should be able to:

PS7   form good relationships with peers and adults

PS8   work as a part of a group or class taking turns and sharing fairly; understanding that there need to be agreed values and codes of behaviour for groups of people, including adults and children, to work harmoniously

PS9   understand what is right, what is wrong and why

PS10   dress and undress independently and manage their own personal hygiene

PS11   select and use activities and resources independently

PS12   consider the consequences of their words and actions for themselves and others

PS13 understand that people have different needs, views, cultures and beliefs which need to be treated with respect

During the topic of Shapes children will work together on several collaborative activities. They will develop skills of listening to each other and taking turns as ideas are shared and preferences expressed. As they share toys and equipment children will learn to think of each others' needs and feelings. Many of the areas outlined above, though, will be covered on an almost incidental basis as children carry out the activities described in this book for the other areas of learning. During undirected free choice times they will be developing independence (PS11) whilst any small group activity which involves working with an adult will help children to build effective relationships (PS7).

Language and Literacy (L)

These goals are in line with the National Literacy Strategy.

Speaking and Listening

By the end of the reception year, most children should be able to:

L1   use language to imagine and recreate roles and experiences

L2   use talk to organise, sequence and clarify thinking, ideas, feelings and events

L3   sustain attentive listening, responding to what they have heard by relevant comments, questions or actions

L4   interact with others negotiating plans and activities and taking turns in conversation

L5   extend their vocabulary exploring the meaning and sounds of new words

L6   retell narratives in the correct sequence drawing on the language pattern of stories

L7   speak clearly and audibly with confidence and control and show awareness of the listener, for example by their use of conventions such as greetings, 'please' and 'thank you'

Reading

By the end of reception most children should be able to:

L8   hear and say initial and final sounds in words and short vowel sounds within words

L9   link letters and sounds, naming and sounding all letters of the alphabet

L10   read a range of familiar and common words and simple sentences independently

L11   show understanding of elements of stories such as main character, sequence of events, opening and how information can be found in non-fiction texts, to answer questions about where, who, why and how

Writing

By the end of reception most children should be able to:

L12   hold a pencil correctly, and form recognisable letters, most of which are correctly formed

L13   use their phonic knowledge to write simple regular words and make phonetically plausible attempts at more complex words

L14   write their own names and labels and form sentences, sometimes using punctuation

L15   attempt writing for various purposes, using features of different forms such as lists, stories, instructions

The activities suggested for the theme of Shapes include several which are based on well-known, quality picture books and stories. They allow children to enjoy listening to the books and to respond in a variety of ways to what they hear, reinforcing and extending their vocabularies. Throughout the topic opportunities are described in which children are encouraged to explore the sounds of words, to use descriptive vocabulary and to see some of their ideas recorded in both pictures and words.

Mathematics (M)

These goals reflect the key objectives in the National Numeracy Strategy.

By the end of reception most children should be able to:

M1 say and use number names in order in familiar contexts

M2 count reliably up to ten everyday objects;

M3 recognise numerals 1 to 9

M4 use language such as 'more' or 'less', 'greater' or 'smaller', 'heavier' or 'lighter' to compare two numbers or quantities

M5 in practical activities and discussion begin to use the vocabulary involved in adding and subtracting

M6 find one more or one less than a number from one to ten

M7 begin to relate addition to combining two groups of objects and subtraction to 'taking away'

M8 talk about, recognise and recreate simple patterns

M9 use language such as 'circle' or 'bigger' to describe the shape and size of solids and flat shapes

M10 use everyday words to describe position

M11 use developing mathematical ideas and methods to solve practical problems

The theme of Shapes provides opportunities for a range of mathematical activities presented in meaningful and practical contexts. A number of them allow children to develop mathematical language and early understandings of both geometrical and irregular shapes. Children are introduced to the concepts of pattern, addition and subtraction, and begin to explore aspects of measure.

Knowledge and Understanding of the World (K)

These goals provide a foundation for scientific, technological, historical and geographical learning.

By the end of reception most children should be able to:

K1 investigate objects and materials by using all of their senses as appropriate

K2 find out about and identify some features of, living things, objects and events they observe

K3 look closely at similarities, differences, patterns and change

K4 ask questions about why things happen and how things work

K5 build and construct with a wide range of objects, selecting appropriate resources and adapting their work where necessary

K6 select tools and techniques they need to shape, assemble and join the materials they are using

K7 find out about and identify the uses of technology in their everyday lives and use computers and programmed toys to support their learning

K8 find out about past and present events in their own lives, and those of their families and other people they know

K9 observe, find out about and identify features in the place where they live and the natural world

K10 find out about their environment and talk about those features they like and dislike

The topic of Shapes offers many opportunities for children to explore and investigate, to make observations and to ask questions. They can extend their awareness of the local environment as they search for shapes and record their findings. They will learn more about the variety of shapes around them, and begin to develop appropriate vocabulary as they describe their observations.

Physical Development (PD)

By the end of reception most children should be able to:

PD1　move with confidence, imagination and in safety

PD2　move with control and co-ordination

PD3　show awareness of space, of themselves and of others

PD4　recognise the importance of keeping healthy and those things which contribute to this

PD5　recognise the changes that happen to their bodies when they are active

PD6　use a range of small and large equipment

PD7　travel around, under, over and through balancing and climbing equipment

PD8　handle tools, objects, construction and malleable materials safely with increasing control.

Through the theme of Shapes children will have opportunities to develop the skills of moving with confidence and imagination. Activities such as working with dough and preparing food will offer experience of working with tools and materials in a practical and purposeful context. Opportunities are taken to encourage control as children play games of throwing and aiming, and more active games give opportunities to draw children's attention to changes in their bodies.

Creative Development (C)

By the end of reception most children should be able to:

C1　explore colour, texture, shape, form and space in two and three dimensions

C2　listen attentively to and explore how sounds can be made louder/quieter, faster/slower, longer/shorter, higher/lower and recognise patterns in music, movement and dance

C3　respond in a variety of ways to what they see, hear, smell, touch and feel

C4　use their imagination in art and design, music, dance, drama, stories and play

C5　express and communicate their ideas, thoughts and feelings by using a widening range of materials, suitable tools, drama, movement, designing and making, and a variety of songs and instruments

During this topic children will experience working with a variety of materials as they print and paint, make models, and explore a range of creative making tasks. Music is used as a way of supporting imaginative movement, with suggestions for the use of pattern in pitch and tempo. Throughout all the activities children are encouraged to talk about what they see and feel as they communicate their ideas in 2D and 3D work, dance, music and role play.

Week 1

Shapes and sizes

Personal, Social and Emotional Development

- Talk about experiences of changing size. Encourage each child to think of a change in their life caused by growth: something they can reach which they couldn't reach before, a favourite ride-on toy they are now too big for or a special item of clothing which they have grown out of. (PS1, 4, 8)

- Start the topic by taking the children shape spotting (see Mathematics activities). Discuss aspects of safety, such as the need to hold hands or stay together. Draw attention to any hazards such as roads or ponds and describe the safety rules associated with these. (PS12)

Language and Literacy

- Tell the story of 'Goldilocks and the Three Bears'. Talk about the different sizes of objects which were found in the bears' house. Encourage children to join in as you tell the story. Sing the song 'When Goldilocks went to the house of the bears' (L3, 5).

- Play 'odd one out' games. Make a collection of objects: building blocks, toys, cut-out shapes, and so on. Present the objects to the children three at a time. In each set of three choose two objects which are similar in shape and one which is different - two spiky shapes and one smooth, two squares and a circle, two circles and a ball. In each case invite children to say which item is the odd one out. Ask them to try to explain how they made their choices. (M4, 9)

Mathematics

- Go for a walk together or look around the room, spotting shapes. Use descriptive vocabulary such as narrow, tall, round, curved, straight, pointed, wiggly, curly and spiky. Draw attention to similar shapes, and make simple comparisons: 'The clock and the plate are both round shapes. Which is bigger?' (M9)

- Make a washing line with examples of clothes of increasing size, from baby clothes through to those which might be worn by members of the group. Talk about the word 'fit'. Encourage children to find pairs of shoes and socks of matching sizes from a collection. (M4)

- Show the children a Russian doll or a set of stacking barrels. Show the children the largest doll or barrel before opening it to reveal a smaller one inside. Encourage the children to predict whether or not there will be yet another inside each doll. Ask the children whether all the objects in the set are the same shape. But are they all the same size? Which are the smallest and largest? Encourage the children to arrange the dolls or barrels in order of size. They can take turns in choosing two dolls from the selection. Which one is smaller? Check by seeing whether or not it will fit inside the larger doll. (M4)

Knowledge and Understanding of the World

- Play shadow games (see activity opposite). (K3)

- Encourage children to explore the use of magnifiers. Talk about the way in which tiny objects appear much larger when viewed through the magnifier. Draw attention to new details which can now be seen. (K1, 2)

- Talk to the children about their own experiences of shapes and sizes. Who can think of a round thing which they see at home or something which is very tall across the street from the school? (K8)

Physical Development

- Play traditional circle games: 'Ring-a-Ring o' Roses, 'Hokey Cokey', 'Farmer's in the Den', 'Here we go Round the Mulberry Bush'. (PD1, 2)

- Use playground chalk to draw a variety of long lines for children to move along. Use zig-zags, wiggly lines, curved lines and straight lines. Ask children to take giant strides along the straight line, take tiny steps along the zig-zag line or skip along the wiggly line. (PD 1)

Creative Development

- Make shape collages. Choose a theme for the collage such as round, square or curly. Provide large paper shapes to use as a base and present a collection of materials designed to illustrate the theme. For example, a curly collage might include pasta spirals, thin strips of coloured curled paper, short lengths of party streamers, curled wrapping ribbon or wood shavings. Older children should be offered one or two inappropriate items to encourage discriminating choices to be made. (C1, 5)

- Make decorated salt dough shapes (see activity below).(C1)

Activity: Shadow games

Learning opportunity: Exploring ways of making different shapes and sizes of shadows.

Early Learning Goal: Knowledge and Understanding of the World. Children should look closely at similarities, differences, patterns and change.

Resources: A sunny day and an outdoor space!

Key vocabulary: Shadow, change, bigger, smaller, spiky, round, tall, short.

Organisation: Whole group.

What to do:

Take the children outside on a sunny day. Stand with them, facing away from the sun, so that the children can see their shadows on the ground in front of them. Encourage the children to lie down with their shadows. Can you run away from your shadow? Is it possible to stand on your shadow?

Set challenges for the children, making shadows as small, tall, wide or thin as possible. Is it possible to make a shadow with no head or no arms?

When children are confident they will be able to work with a friend, making monsters with two heads and three legs!

Activity: Decorated salt dough shapes

Learning opportunity: Working imaginatively with a malleable material.

Early Learning Goal: Creative Development. Children should explore colour, texture, shape, form and space in two and three dimensions.

Resources: A batch of salt dough made by mixing the following ingredients:

- 2 bags plain flour
- 1 bag salt
- 4 tablespoons oil
- water to mix
- Colouring (optional)
- Rolling pins; safe knives; small cutters; brushes; small water pot.

Key vocabulary: Square, round, straight, wavy, curly.

Organisation: Small groups.

What to do:

Show the children how to roll out the dough and to use the safe knives and cutters to cut shapes from the dough. Additional shapes can be used to decorate. Use a damp brush to join pieces of dough when modelling. If a small hole is made near the edge of the shape, a ribbon can later be threaded through it to make a hanging decoration.

Bake the results very slowly - overnight in an only just warm oven is best. The models can be painted after baking.

Display

Make a collection of interesting objects for children to look at through a magnifier: newspaper pictures, bark, moss, open-weave fabric, pieces of wood. It is worth saving the type of greeting card boxes which have clear acetate lids. These are useful for displaying delicate objects for children to look at without handling. Magnifiers can be attached to ribbons to keep them in the display area.

Week 2

Patterns

Personal, Social and Emotional Development

- Read the story of *Elmer* by David McKee. Discuss Elmer's difficulties and the happy ending of the story. (PS13)

- Explain to the children that they are going to be looking at patterns. What sort of patterns do they like? Show them a collection of wrapping paper. Which patterns do they think would be suitable for different occasions or people? Look at a range of wallpaper samples. Which would they like in their bedrooms? Which patterns would be suitable for friends or other family members? Encourage the children to talk about preferences and express opinions. (PS4)

Language and Literacy

- As you look at the patterned papers (see above) encourage children to develop vocabulary which describes colours, shapes and patterns, including checks, stripes or spots. (L5)

- After listening to stories about Elmer, encourage children to design their own patterns to draw on to prepared elephant shapes. Let them give names to their elephants and tell you about the patterns they have chosen for them. (L2)

- Encourage auditory skills by challenging children to join in as you make sound patterns. Start by making body sound patterns: clap, clap, tap; clap, clap, tap; clap, clap, tap. Progress to making patterns of phonemes: ch, ch, p; ch, ch, p; ch, ch, p. Can children make their own sound patterns for others to copy? (L3, 8)

- Read stories with repetitive structures which enable children to join in as familiar phrases constantly recur. Good examples are 'The Enormous Turnip', 'The Gingerbread Man' (both Ladybird Books)and 'The Elephant and the Bad Baby' by Elfrida Vipont published by Puffin. (L3, 6)

Mathematics

- Make a series of games using patterned papers (see activity opposite). (M8, 11)

- Encourage children to make patterns using bright finger paints on black paper. Talk about straight, curved and wavy lines, spots, dots and stripes, squares, triangles, stars and circles. (M9)

- Print on to dough using everyday items such as spoons, cotton reels, wheels and Lego bricks. Encourage the children to make predictions. What sort of shape will this make in the dough? Can other children guess which item made each print? (M9)

Knowledge and Understanding of the World

- Make simple kaleidoscopes (see activity opposite). (K3)

- Make a record of different patterns and textures from the immediate environment. Explore different techniques: making wax crayon rubbings of tree bark, copying the pattern of brickwork using Lego bricks, printing the pattern of paving stones using shaped sponges or recreating the herringbone pattern of wooden block flooring using oblongs of paper. (K2, 5, 9)

Physical Development

- If your group has access to ride-on toys, make a large puddle of water outside. Encourage children to ride slowly through the puddle and then make wet track patterns as they ride about. If you don't have any ride-on toys, give children brushes and brooms to use in painting large water patterns outside on a sunny day. (PD6, 8)

- Make a course using simple apparatus to encourage different movement patterns. Make a slalom line of cones through which children weave, a circle of bean bags to skip around and a zig-zag line of hoops to jump along. (PD1, 2, 3, 6)

- Work with children in creating repeating patterns of movement: jump, jump, clap; jump, jump, clap. Encourage them to design their own simple movement patterns to share with others. (PD2)

Creative Development

- Make welly prints. Ask each child to bring in a pair of wellington boots. Place a long piece of paper (wallpaper is ideal) on the floor. At one end of the paper an adult helps the child to stand on a large sponge covered in ready-mixed paint. The child's hand is held as they walk along the paper to where another helper is waiting with a bowl of soapy water to wash the wellies. Look at the patterns made by different treads and the different tracks of long and short steps. (C1)

- Encourage children to recognise and move to different musical patterns: high and low notes, long and short notes, fast and slow music. (C2)

Activity: Patterned paper games

Learning opportunity: Recognising and describing patterns and using this in a game.

Early Learning Goal: Mathematics. Children should talk about and recognise ...... simple patterns; and use developing mathematical ideas and methods to solve practical problems.

Resources: Pieces of wallpaper and wrapping paper; card.

Key vocabulary: Same, different, pair.

Organisation: Small group.

What to do:

Pattern snap: Make a set of cards using the paper scraps. Make four cards with samples of each pattern. (About six sets of four cards is plenty.) Use the cards for children to play a snap matching game.

Picking pairs: Spread the cards from the previous activity face down on the floor or a table top. Children take turns in turning over two cards, looking for pairs, which are then stored at one side until all the cards are turned over.

Kim's game: Place three or four cards face up on the table. Cover with a cloth and remove one. Can the children describe the missing card?

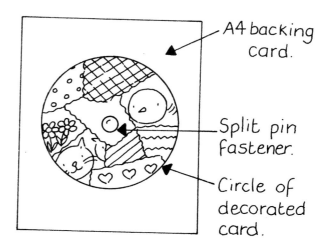

A4 backing card.

Split pin fastener.

Circle of decorated card.

Activity: A simple kaleidoscope

Learning opportunity: Watching patterns change as they are turned between mirrors.

Early Learning Goal: Knowledge and Understanding of the World. Children should look closely at ... patterns and change.

Resources: Shopping catalogues; sheets of A4 card and card circles; plastic flat mirrors or rectangles of good quality mirrored card; glue; scissors; split pin fasteners.

Key vocabulary: Reflection, pattern.

Organisation: Small group.

What to do:

Provide each child with a circle of card, large enough to just fit on a piece of A4 paper. Show them how to cut busy pictures out of shopping catalogues or magazines and to stick them all over the circle.

Gently bend the covered circle into four to locate the centre and push a split pin fastener through the centre. Fix this to a piece of A4 card, checking that it rotates freely around the split pin fastener.

Hold two mirrors at an angle to each other above the centre split pin and as the child turns the decorated circle, amazing patterns will appear as reflections.

Display

Make a display of patterns from the environment recorded by the children. Can visitors identify the source and location of the original surfaces?

Week 3
Holes

Personal, Social and Emotional Development

- Pass a piece of card with a 10p piece sized hole in it around the group. Children take turns in using it peep-show fashion, describing what they can see - imaginary responses are as valuable as real ones! Talk about the importance of taking turns and of listening to each other. This activity is best carried out in short sessions repeated over the week until all the children who wish to have had a turn. (PS1,2,8)

- Talk about buttons and button holes. Have a selection of garments available for children to practise their buttoning skills. Encourage children to practise on their own clothes as appropriate. (PS10)

Language and Literacy

- Read the story books *Peepo!* and *The Very Hungry Caterpillar*. Both these books have holes in the pages which are integral to the stories. (L3)

- Using thin card, cut out an initial letter shape for each child. Use a hole punch to make holes about 2 cm apart all around the edges. Provide brightly coloured wools and show children how to decorate their initial letters by threading the wools through the holes. (L14)

Mathematics

- Play with shape sorting 'posting' toys, encouraging children to make predictions about the shapes which will fit through each hole in the toy. (M9)

- Make a hole in the top of a shoe box. Use this as a resource in developing early number skills. With the children, count up to three small toys as you post them into the box. Ask the children to tell you how many toys are in the box. Remove the lid to check. Replace the lid and post in another toy. How many are in the box now? Again, make a final check by opening the box. (M6, 7)

Knowledge and Understanding of the World

- Talk about animals which live in holes in the ground. Partially fill the sand tray with peat or compost and provide appropriate toy animals, a few pebbles, leaves and small twigs. Encourage children to 'find' animals in the ground and to make burrows and dens for them. (K2)

- Equip the water tray with a selection of containers with holes in them: colanders, plastic flower pots, sieves, watering cans, slotted spoons. Talk about the different ways in which water pours through the holes. Introduce appropriate vocabulary such as tip, pour, sprinkle, full, empty. (K2, 4)

- Blow bubbles using a variety of objects with holes, or blowers shaped from plastic covered wire. Does the shape of the hole affect the shape of the bubbles? Which blowers give the biggest/most bubbles? (K1, 3, 4)

Physical Development

- Make a scoring game (see activity opposite). (PD2)

- Hold a PE hoop at right angles to the ground for children to climb through. Make the game more challenging by asking adults to stand in line, making a series of holes for children to negotiate. (PD7)

Creative Development

- Make a peep show (see activity opposite). (C5)

- Lay a stencil on paper, and dip an old toothbrush

in some ready mixed paint. Show children how to flick the brush over the holes in the stencil to spatter paint. Lift away the stencil to reveal a painted shape beneath. (C1)

Activity: Make a scoring game

Learning opportunity: Children will develop aiming skills.

Early Learning Goal: Physical Development. Children should move with control and co-ordination.

Resources: Large cardboard grocery boxes; paint; large brushes; paper; scissors; soft balls.

Key vocabulary: Throw, aim, score.

Organisation: Small group.

What to do:

Stand each cardboard box on one of its sides and cut out a large hole (almost enough to make the box look like a television screen). Cover the remaining surfaces of the box and allow children to decorate with paint.

Stand the boxes at some distance from the children and encourage them to aim soft balls through the holes. Move the boxes further away as children gain confidence.

To make the game into a scoring game, place some boxes nearer than others, or make some holes larger than others.

Activity: Make a peep-show

Learning opportunity: Making a peep-show using different materials.

Early Learning Goal: Creative Development. Children should express and communicate their ideas, thoughts and feelings by using a widening range of materials, suitable tools and designing and making.

Resources: Shoe boxes or cereal boxes; variety of papers; greetings cards; tissue paper; cards and decorative materials; scissors; glue.

Key vocabulary: Cut, stick, view, hole.

Organisation: Small group.

What to do:

Take the lids from the shoe boxes, or remove one of the large sides from the cereal boxes. Help the children to cut a small hole, about the size of a 2p piece in one of the shorter ends of the box.

Show the children how to cut pictures from the greetings cards. By folding up a small gluing flap at the bottom of each picture they can be stuck to the 'floor' inside the box to gradually build up a scene. Demonstrate how to ensure that all the pictures face the hole in the box wall.

Cover the open surface of the box with tissue paper. Show the children how to peep through the hole in the side of the box to see the scene they have created.

Display

Make an interactive peep-show display. Line a large but shallow grocery box with plain coloured paper.

Stick a number of bright, simple pictures, or attach a number of small but familiar objects into the bottom of the box. Cover the box with tissue paper and carefully use a felt tip pen to mark the position of each picture or object. Remove the tissue paper but save it. Fasten the bottom of the box, at child height, onto a wall using strong pins. Cover it with thin card or thick paper. Place the tissue paper you marked earlier on top of this. Use the felt pen marks to show you where to cut small holes about 2 cm across in the box's cover. Fix the cover in place and invite children to peep through the holes to see what is in the box.

Week 4

Tubes

Personal, Social and Emotional Development

- Show the children an empty sweet tube. Tell them a story about the tube of sweets and about all the people who enjoyed sharing them. Use this as a stimulus to encourage children to talk about their own experiences of sharing; sweets, toys, games. (PS7, 8, 9, 12)

Language and Literacy

- Develop listening skills by playing a version of Chinese whispers. Pass a cardboard tube, for example from a kitchen roll, around the group. Each child whispers down the tube, passing a message to the child next to them. (L3, 4)

- Make a cylinder finger puppet show (see activity opposite). (L1)

- Tell a story of a magic tube. Many children will have seen or enjoyed tubular chutes at swimming pools. Sliding down the magic chute grants special wishes! It can also change people into anything they want to be. Invite the children to talk about what their choices might be. (L2, 4)

Mathematics

- Introduce the word cylinder as another word for a straight tube. The ends of the cylinder can be either open or closed. Show a variety of cylinders: building blocks, cardboard tubes, drinking straws, snack packaging. Introduce comparative language: smaller, bigger, shorter, longer, wider, narrower. (M9)

- Prepare a printing tube by using a strong glue (such as from a glue gun) to fix some string in a random pattern over the surface of a sturdy cardboard cylinder. Use the tube to make impressions as children roll it over soft dough. Encourage the children also to try pressing the ends of the cylinder into the dough and draw attention to the identical round shapes made by either end. (M9)

- Develop counting skills using a cardboard tube which has been covered in shiny paper. Drop marbles, counters or small plastic animals down the tube and encourage the children to count them as they emerge at the other end. (M1, 2)

Knowledge and Understanding of the World

- Provide funnels, clear tubes and pouring toys in the water tray. Add food colouring to the water so it can be seen travelling through the tubes. (K1)

- Make listening tubes. Firmly press the stem of a large plastic funnel into each end of a long tube or length of hosepipe. Even whispered sounds travel effectively for long distances. The tube does not need to be either taut or straight. (K2, 4)

- Talk about any tunnels close by which the children may have seen. Some children may have travelled on tube trains or journeyed in a car through a long tunnel. Did they enjoy this experience? Place some old toy cars in a tray of wet sand and encourage the children to make tunnels for them to travel through. (K5, 9, 10)

- Make a ramp down which children can roll cylinders. Does making the ramp steeper make any difference to the distance rolled? (K4)

Physical Development

- Provide tubes and tunnels for children to crawl through. Make your own by draping old sheets over appropriate, safe supports. (PD7)

- Make an aiming game in which children roll balls of tightly screwed paper down cardboard tubes. Mark target rings on the floor using chalk. (PD2)

Creative Development

- Make a tubular orchestra (see activity opposite). (C5)

- Colour macaroni by shaking dry pasta in a bag with a little food colouring. Slowly dry on a piece of non-stick parchment in a gentle oven. Thread the coloured macaroni to make necklaces. (C1)

- Do blow painting. Place a largish blob of runny paint near the bottom of a sheet of paper. Children hold drinking straws just above the paper to blow the paint along. (Holding the straw almost parallel to the paper gets the best results.) (C5)

- Use drinking straws to blow into a mixture of watered down paint and washing-up liquid in a small bowl or margarine pot. Lay paper on top of the bubbles to make a print. (C1)

- Build with construction straws. (C1)

Activity: A cylinder finger puppet show

Learning opportunity: Acting out imaginative situations.

Early Learning Goal: Language and Literacy. Children should use language to imagine and recreate roles and experiences.

Resources: Pre-cut rectangles of thin card (about 8 x 5 cm); paper and decorative scraps; greetings cards; felt pens; scissors; glue; adhesive tape.

Key vocabulary: Roll, cut, stick, cylinder, puppet.

Organisation: Small group.

What to do:

Start to make the puppets by working with the rectangle of card. Help the children to mark the approximate mid-point of the card. This will be the front of their puppet.

Talk about how to decide on the character which they want to make. Older or more able children will be able to draw their own faces, but younger children will find it more satisfying to cut faces and characters from greetings cards to stick to their puppets.

Further decoration can be added before the card is rolled into a finger sized cylinder. Trim as necessary and fix with adhesive tape.

Encourage the children to play with their puppets, developing situations and holding conversations.

Activity: A tubular orchestra

Learning opportunity: Making and using instruments.

Early Learning Goal: Creative Development. Children should express and communicate their ideas using a widening range of materials, suitable tools and a variety of instruments.

Resources: Lidded cylindrical potato snack containers; long wide tubes; plastic tubing; funnels; bowls; beans; rice; sand; strong elastic bands; paper; decorative materials; scissors, glue.

Key vocabulary: Shake, tip, fill, sound, loud, soft, quiet, gentle.

Organisation: Small group.

What to do:

Make a variety of instruments as follows:

Snack box shakers
Show the children how to place a handful of beans inside a cylindrical snack container. Replace the lid. Help them to cover the container with paper and decorate.

These tubes have metal at one end and a plastic lid at the other, Gently tipping the contents from end to end results in two different sounds. The ends can also be tapped to produce more variety.

Sea-side sounds
Cover one end of a long, wide tube (a postal tube is ideal) with paper held by a tight elastic band. Tip in a yogurt potful of dry sand or rice. Cover the end as before and decorate the outside of the tube. Slowly tip the tube from end to end to produce a gentle wave-like sound.

Water sounds
To add watery sounds to a performance fix a funnel firmly into one end of a clear plastic tube. Listen to the sounds as water is poured into the funnel and runs into a bowl. Encourage children to experiment with ways of changing the sounds made.

Display

Decorate a display board to resemble a puppet theatre by placing draped paper curtains at either side and adding a pleated paper pelmet curtain across the top. Use this as both storage and display for the cylinder puppets.

Make a space scene display. Cut bubble prints into round shapes and stick to a black background. Add a few cylinder rockets made from covered cardboard tubes.

Week 5

Boxes

Personal, Social and Emotional Development

- Play 'Pass the box'. A cardboard box is passed around the group. Each child in turn pretends to take something from the box and describes it to the rest of the group who guess its identity. For example: 'I have found something soft and furry in the box. It is something alive. It has long ears and a twitchy nose'. After a small number of children have had a turn, put the box away and continue the game on another occasion, to prevent children sitting for too long awaiting turns. (PS2, 8)

Language and Literacy

- Develop positional language using a small toy and a lidded box. Use the toy as a naughty friend who climbs and hides. Ask the children to tell you whether the toy is under the box, inside the box, behind the box in front of the box or on top of the box. (L5)

- Say together this traditional action rhyme. As children become familiar with the rhyme encourage them to offer ideas for the contents of the box. (L3)

Here is a box	(Make a fist with one hand - the box)
And here's the lid.	(Place the other hand on top of the fist - the lid)
I wonder what inside is hid?	
I think it's a .... without a doubt.	(Insert name of animal, vehicle.......)
Let's open the box	(Lift hand lid)
And let it come out.	(Children make appropriate animal or vehicle sound)

- Use a box again to encourage recognition of initial sounds. Hide a small object in the box and play an 'I-spy' based game in which children guess what is in the box.

  Here is a box with something inside

  What do you think it is?

  It begins with a ....   (Insert initial sound)

  Can you decide?

  What do you think it is?

Mathematics

- Make a shape shopping game (see activity opposite). (M11)

- Place a selection of objects of different weights inside similar sized boxes. Can the children order the boxes from lightest to heaviest? (M11)

- Develop ordinal number recognition. Make a line of five boxes each containing a different small toy. Label the boxes first to fifth. Use the ordinal number names in talking to the children. 'What do you think is in the first box?' and so on. Once all the boxes are emptied give instructions using ordinal number names to refill the boxes. For example, 'Put the toy elephant in the third box'. (M1)

- Use packaging boxes for modelling. As children use the different boxes, talk about their shapes and properties. Point out any unusual shapes, bigger and smaller boxes, square faces and so on. (M11)

Knowledge and Understanding of the World

- Talk about special boxes, such as treasure chests, jewellery boxes and so on, and what might be inside them. Use this to introduce the idea of a time capsule. What might the children choose to put in a time capsule box which would tell someone else about where they live and what they do? (K8, 9, 10)

- Explore materials through decorating lidded cardboard boxes. (Round cheese boxes are ideal.) Choose a theme for the boxes - natural materials, shiny materials - and provide a selection of appropriate decorating materials which children can glue to the lids. Introduce and reinforce relevant vocabulary as the children work. If natural materials are used, talk about where they may have been found. (K2)

Physical Development

- Make a target throwing game in which children aim bean bags into boxes. (PD2)

- Use Jack-in-the-Box toys as a starting point for a miming activity in which children start by silently crouching on the floor until a given signal is given when they jump up and clap. (PD1)

Creative Development

- Encourage children to work together in making a model village (see activity below). (C4)

- Encourage dance and role play by imagining a huge magic toy box. As you take various items from the box children move in an appropriate way, for example toy soldier, robot, train, clown, doll. (C4)

Activity: The shape shopping game

Learning opportunity: Developing strategies to solve a puzzle.

Early Learning Goal: Mathematics. Children should use mathematical ideas and methods to solve practical problems.

Resources: A large dice; paper and Blu-tack; a variety of packaging containers.

Key vocabulary: Same, different, taller, shorter, round, straight, cube, cuboid, cylinder.

Organisation: Small group.

What to do:

Stick paper labels on the sides of the dice to show 2 x cuboids, 2 x cylinders, 1 x cube, 1 x ?

Make a shop with the empty grocery containers. Children take it in turns to roll the dice and to select a package which matches the shape they have thrown. Throwing a question mark allows a free choice and accommodates odd shapes such as prisms. Through the activity children should discover that cuboids come in all shapes and sizes, and that cylinders may be the shape of a snack box or a round cheese box.

Activity: Making a model village

Learning opportunity: Working collaboratively to make a model village.

Early Learning Goal: Creative Development. Children should use their imagination in art and design, music, dance, drama, stories and play.

Resources: Large floor area. Wide variety of modelling kits - blocks, construction kits, mini-world toys, toy vehicles, recycled materials.

Key vocabulary: House, street, playground, trees and so on.

Organisation: Large group.

What to do:

Explain to the children that they are all going to work together to make a large model of a village or town. Talk to the children about the sorts of buildings and areas which they will need to build. Give responsibility for different areas to different children: playground, park, school, market and so on.

Encourage the children to work together building roads, streets and play areas. Encourage them to use a variety of materials, incorporating toy vehicles or people to add realism. Allow the children to think of other materials they can use - green paper for grass, a sand area, railway set.

Join in the imaginative play suggesting new ideas and creating role play situations such as a lorry which tips up, blocking the road.

Display

Make a large background of a box decorated as a parcel. Arrange cut-out figures around the box to illustrate prepositions: put a picture of a mouse under the box, one of a cat on top of the box and so on. Add the appropriate prepositions as captions. Invite children to suggest 'What might be inside the box?'

Week 6

The Great Shape Show

Personal, Social and Emotional Development

- Explain to the children that you will be holding an event to which families and friends will be invited. There will be plenty to do to get ready. Everyone will need to work together to help. Involve the children in planning the event and in making decisions about choices of food. (PS7, 13)

- Encourage the children to think about the activities which they have carried out over the past few weeks. Which ones might visitors like to try? Ask the children in turn to think of their favourites. Talk about the need to listen to each other with courtesy and to appreciate that people have different opinions and preferences. (PS8)

Language and Literacy

- Talk to the children about the types of food and drink which they will be serving at the Great Shape Show. Explain that it is helpful to label food so that guests know what it is that they are being offered! Show the children how to make simple label flags for food using paper and blunted cocktail sticks. Encourage the children to decorate flags with pre-cut, drawn or gummed shapes, with older or more able children helping to write the names of the items. (L12, 14,15)

- Make posters and invitations for the show. (L15)

Mathematics

- Make clown shape masks to wear at the show. Use paper plates as the basis of the masks, helping children by drawing the position of eye-holes and starting off the cutting process. Decorate the masks with assorted shapes. Talk to the children about the shapes being used and the patterns on the mask which they are making. More able children will enjoy exploring symmetry. Add wool or coloured cotton wool hair and a card triangular hat. Use a hole punch to make attachments for ribbon or hat elastic. (M8, 9, 10)

- Picture shape building games (see activity opposite). (M11)

- Make a matching game to share with visitors in which coloured pictures of objects have to be matched to their outlines in black paper. Make the game using simple wooden templates. Children draw and cut out two versions of each shape, one on black, and one on white paper which is then coloured and decorated. (M9)

Knowledge and Understanding of the World

- Put out a collection of leaves to stimulate conversations with visitors about shape. Ask children to talk about and compare the size of the leaves and their shapes: pointed, round, long. Introduce words to describe the outer edges of the leaves: straight, wavy or jagged. Show children one leaf and ask them to find another which has the same shape, or a similar edge. (K2, 3)

- Make a shape guessing game. Place a selection of objects on an overhead projector table. Can children help their guests guess what the objects are from their projected shadows? (K1)

- Make a magnetic shape fishing game. Cut out a number of shapes from coloured paper and fix a paper-clip to the corner of each. Devise a scoring system as visitors (with the help of children) fish for the shapes using magnet rods. (K2, 4)

- Fill shaped containers with fruit juice to make unusual ice cubes. (K3)

Physical Development

- Play follow my leader, making different body shapes as you move around the room. Sometimes walk in straight lines, sometimes in wavy lines and sometimes as though on a zig-zag line. (PD2, 3)

- Practise playing musical shapes, a variation of musical statues. Music is played as the children dance. When the music stops an adjective is called out describing the shape the children should make: spiky, wide, thin, flat, round, small. No one ever needs to be out of the game which is played simply for enjoyment! (PD1, 2, 3)

Creative Development

- Show children how to make their own jigsaw puzzles by cutting up picture cards. Explain that about four pieces is usually enough to make a puzzle! Place the completed puzzles on display at the Great Shape Show for guests to have a go. (C1)

- Provide materials for children to help their guests make shape party hats. Cut long paper strips with an assortment of wavy or zig-zag edges, and decorate with pre-cut or gummed paper shapes, sequins and glue. (C1, 5)

- Make party box cakes. Cut a slab cake into squares to make roughly cube-shaped pieces. Show the children how to cover these with ready-made rolled fondant icing. Decorate with coloured sweets and red liquorice ribbon. (C1, 5)

- Use collage materials to decorate giant squares, circles, hearts, diamonds and so on. Use them as decorations at the Great Shape Show. (C1, 4)

Activity: Posters and Invitations

Learning opportunity: Using writing for a real purpose.

Early Learning Goal: Language and Literacy. Children should attempt writing for various purposes.

Resources: Paper; pens; envelopes; crayons and a selection of writing materials.

Key vocabulary: Date, time, day, invitation.

Organisation: Small group.

What to do:

Making posters:
Explain to the children that guests will need to know about their event. Talk to the children about the types of information which guests will need. When is the event to be held? Where is it? At what times will it begin and end? Will refreshments be served? Talk about the need to present this information clearly and simply.

Record the children's ideas and write them in the centre of a sheet of A4 paper. Make several photocopies of the poster, enlarging to A3 if possible.

Invite children to add their own shape designs to the poster designs. Talk about the need for designs to be bright and eye catching.

Invitations:
Children may wish to make sure that their own friends and families attend the event by issuing invitations. These offer more opportunities for new writers to practise their skills.

Having discussed the information which should be on the invitation, photocopy a template for children to complete. Leave spaces for children to fill in the names of the person to be invited, and their own names as senders.

Again, encourage decoration of borders. Place the

invitations in envelopes to encourage more writing. Requesting replies will allow children to receive letters, which will reinforce the importance of reading within a real context.

Activity: Make a shape picture building game

Learning opportunity: Matching and using shapes.

Early Learning Goal: Mathematics. Children should use language such as 'circle' or 'bigger' to describe the shape and size of solids and flat shapes.

Resources: Pattern blocks or plastic mosaics; a dice; A4 card.

Key vocabulary: Round, square, diamond, oblong, triangle, hexagon and so on, appropriate to the set of blocks used.

Organisation: Small group.

What to do:

The aim of this game is to collect pattern blocks to cover a prepared picture. The shapes are won by throwing a dice.

Cover the sides of a large dice with pictures of the pattern blocks for example 1 x diamond, 1 x triangle, 1 x square, 1 x oblong, 2 x ?

Prepare a number of picture cards, making designs and patterns by drawing around the pattern blocks or plastic mosaics available. Each card should have the same total number of shapes on it, and a similar range of different shapes. (It would be difficult, by the laws of chance, to complete a picture which was, for example, made entirely of triangles.)

Throwing a question mark allows any shape to be selected, which can help the game to move more quickly, especially towards the end.

Display:

Display exploding shapes with copies of the original outlines from which they were made. Can children match the old and new versions? (Exploding shapes are like jigsaw pieces moved out in an exploding pattern so that there are gaps between all the pieces.)

Bringing it all together

Introducing The Great Shape Show

Explain to the children that they are going to invite friends and families to join them for an event. They will be enjoying shape activities together, and showing some of the work they have been doing.

Encourage the children to think about some of the activities they have enjoyed during the previous weeks. Which do they think their families and friends might like to try?

Further activity ideas

- **Make a shape hunting game**

  Prepare a large number of pairs of cards. Each card in the pair has an identical shape or pattern on it. Hide one of each pair around the room or, if appropriate, in a safe outdoor area. The remaining cards are given to individuals or small groups of children one at a time. The children hunt for the matching card. When they find it they take it to an adult. In return they are given a card from a different pair with the challenge to find its partner. The game continues until all the pairs of cards are found.

- **Hold a tower building contest**

  Visitors all try their hand at stacking wooden blocks to build a tower. Offer a small prize or certificate for the tallest tower or largest number of blocks used.

- Entertain guests with performances from the cylinder finger-puppet theatre and the tubular band!

Involving the children in preparations

Making refreshments

- Use shaped cutters when preparing sandwiches. Decorate cakes and biscuits with jelly shapes, round chocolate buttons or tiny dolly mixtures.

- Include some commercially produced cakes which have a strong shape connection: Battenburg slices, Swiss roll slices or chocolate rolls (almost cylindrical!)

- Slice fruit in different ways, making circles of apple, triangles of orange and so on, to add to fruit drinks.

- Make a castle cake as a centrepiece for the event. Start with a square sponge cake. Add a Swiss roll tower at each corner. Cover with butter icing. Add chocolate finger biscuit windows and a rectangular biscuit door. Children can make flags decorated with shapes to add to the turrets.

Accessories

- Make two slits in brightly coloured paper shapes. Thread drinking straws through the slits to make cocktail stirrers.

- Buy a plain paper tablecloth and let the children help you decorate it with printed shapes.

Resources

Resources to collect

- Wallpaper remnants.
- Wrapping paper.
- Old greetings cards.
- Large dice.
- Strong mirrored card or plastic flat mirrors.
- Split pin fasteners.

Everyday resources

- Boxes, large and small, for modelling.
- Papers and cards of different weights, colours and textures, such as sugar paper, corrugated card, silver and shiny papers.
- Dry powder paints for mixing and mixed paints for covering large areas.
- Different sized paint brushes from household brushes to thin brushes for delicate work and a variety of paint mixing containers.
- A variety of drawing and colouring pencils, crayons, pastels, charcoals and chalks.
- Additional decorative and finishing materials such as sequins, foils, glitter, tinsel, shiny wool and threads, beads, pieces of textiles, parcel ribbon.
- Paper table covers.

Stories

Miss Brick the Builder's Baby by Allan Ahlberg and Colin McNaughton (Puffin Books).

Rumble in the Jungle by Giles Andeae and David Wojtowycz (Orchard Books).

Noah's Ark by Lucy Cousins (Walker Books).

The Blue Balloon by Mick Inkpen (Hodder Children's Books).

Elmer by David McKee (Red Fox).

Elmer and the Lost Teddy by David McKee (Andersen Press).

Elmer and the Wind by David McKee (Andersen Press).

Elmer and Wilbur by David McKee (Red Fox).

Billy's Box; Nishal's Box; Sophie's Box; Tom's Box; Vicky's Box; Yasmin's Box all by John Prater (Cambridge University Press).

Can You Spot the Spotty Dog? A Hide-and-Seek Book by John Rowe (Red Fox).

The Leopard's Drum by Jessica Souhami (Frances Lincoln).

The Gingerbread Man (Ladybird Books).

The Enormous Turnip (Ladybird Books).

The Elephant and the Bad Baby by Elfrida Vipont (Puffin).

Peepo! by Janet and Allan Ahlberg (Kestrel Books).

The Very Hungry Caterpillar by Eric Carle (Picture Puffin).

Non-fiction

Bear in a Square by Stella Blackstone (Barefoot Books).

The Shape of Things by Dayle Ann Dodds (Walker Books).

Fun to Learn Shapes by Arianne Holden (Lorenz Books).

Fun With Maths - Shapes and Solids by Lakshmi Hewavisenti (Gloucester Press).

First Book of Shapes and Colours by Neil Morris (Dempsey Park).

Readabout Wheels by Henry Pluckrose (Franklin Watts).

Oranges and Lemons, Singing and Dancing Games by Ian Beck and Karen King (Oxford University Press).

Poems and rhymes

This Little Puffin by Elizabeth Matterson (Puffin).

Collecting evidence of children's learning

Monitoring children's development is an important task. Keeping a record of children's achievements will help you to see progress and will draw attention to those who are having difficulties for some reason. If a child needs additional professional help, such as speech therapy, your records will provide valuable evidence.

Records should be the result of collaboration between group leaders, parents and carers. Parents should be made aware of your record keeping policies when their child joins your group. Show them the type of records you are keeping and make sure they understand that they have an opportunity to contribute. As a general rule, your records should form an open document. Any parent should have access to records relating to his or her child. Take regular opportunities to talk to parents about children's progress. If you have formal discussions regarding children about whom you have particular concerns, a dated record of the main points should be kept.

Keeping it manageable

Records should be helpful in informing group leaders, adult helpers and parents and always be for the benefit of the child. However, keeping records of every aspect of each child's development can become a difficult task. The sample shown will help to keep records manageable and useful. The golden rule is to keep them simple.

Observations will fall into three categories:

- **Spontaneous records:** Sometimes you will want to make a note of observations as they happen, for example a child is heard counting cars accurately during a play activity, or is seen to play collaboratively for the first time.

- **Planned observations:** Sometimes you will plan to make observations of children's developing skills in their everyday activities. Using the learning opportunity identified for an activity will help you to make appropriate judgements about children's capabilities and to record them systematically.

To collect information:
- talk to children about their activities and listen to their responses;
- listen to children talking to each other;
- observe children's work such as early writing, drawings, paintings and 3D models. (Keeping photocopies or photographs is sometimes useful.)

Sometimes you may wish to set up 'one off' activities for the purposes of monitoring development. Some groups, for example, ask children to make a drawing of themselves at the beginning of each term to record their progressing skills in both co-ordination and observation. Do not attempt to make records following every activity!

- **Reflective observations:** It is useful to spend regular time reflecting on the progress of a few children (say four each week). Aim to make some brief comments about each child every half term.

Informing your planning

Collecting evidence about children's progress is time consuming and it is important that it is useful. When you are planning, use the information you have collected to help you decide what learning opportunities you need to provide next for children. For example, a child who has poor pencil or brush control will benefit from more play with dough or construction toys to build the strength of hand muscles.

Example of recording chart

Name: Lucy Copson		D.O.B. 26.2.96		Date of entry: 13.9.99	
Term	**Personal, Social, Emotional**	**Language and Literacy**	**Mathematics**	**Knowledge and Understanding**	**Physical**	**Creative**
ONE	Reluctant to say good bye to mother. Prefers adult company 20.9.99 EMH	Enjoying listening to stories. *Elephant and the Bad Baby* a particular favourite 20.11.99 EMH	Is able to say numbers to ten and to count accurately five objects. Recognises and names squares and circles. 5.11.99 BM	Enjoyed using magnifier. Is able to talk about places near home. 16.10.99 AC	Can balance on one leg. Finds stacking blocks difficult. 16.10.99 AC	Enjoys gluing and cutting. Made a wonderful model robot. 20.10.99 LSS
TWO						
THREE						

Skills overview of six week plan

Week	Topic focus	Personal, Social and Emotional	Language and Literacy	Mathematics	Knowledge and Understanding of the World	Physical	Creative
1	Shape and sizes	Sharing experiences Safety awareness	Developing vocabulary Describing observations	Comparative language Naming shapes	Making observations	Moving with control and imagination	Using malleable materials Cutting
2	Patterns	Discussing preferences Sensitivity to others	Listening to stories Discussing Initial sounds	Describing size and shape Repeating patterns	Making observations Recording	Using large apparatus	Printing Musical patterns Dance
3	Holes	Taking turns Dressing independently	Listening to stories Making predictions Initial sounds	Matching shapes Early number skills	Observing Describing Talking	Moving with control Aiming	Using materials imaginatively Painting
4	Tubes	Sharing	Listening Retelling stories	Language of shape Pattern Counting	Listening Talking Investigating Observing	Aiming Using large apparatus	Making and using instruments Painting Constructing
5	Boxes	Taking turns Describing feelings Listening to others	Rhyme Initial sounds Developing language	Identifying shapes Measure Ordinal numbers	Time awareness Exploring materials	Aiming Miming	Collaborative modelling Dance Role play
6	The Great Shape Show	Sharing responsibility Preparing for an event	Writing for a purpose	Shape awareness	Observing change	Moving with an awareness of others	Collage Using foods Making for a purpose

Home links

The theme of Shapes lends itself to useful links with children's homes and families. Through working together children and adults gain respect for each other and build comfortable and confident relationships.

Establishing partnerships

- Keep parents informed about the topic of Shapes, and the themes for each week. By understanding the work of the group, parents will enjoy the involvement of contributing ideas, time and resources.

- Photocopy the parent's page for each child to take home.

- Invite friends, childminders and families to share all or part of the Great Shape Show event.

Visiting enthusiasts

- Ask the local librarian to come into the group to read relevant stories or poems. Ask whether any parents or friends who are interested in cake decoration would show the children some techniques in decorating cakes or biscuits with shapes.

Resource requests

- Ask parents to contribute any fabric scraps, buttons, ribbons, trimmings or parcel decorations which are no longer needed.

- Wallpaper or wrapping paper scraps will be useful in providing examples of pattern.

- Boxes for the peep shows, cheese boxes to decorate and other clean packaging will be needed throughout this theme.

- Ask to borrow shaped ice-cube containers or cake tins.

Preparing the event

- It is always useful to have extra adults at events, and support in preparing food will be especially welcome.